MW00462783

In the Quiet Spaces

Copyright 2016 by
Clarence Young

$8.99

Print ISBN 978-0-692-80628-9
Obsidian Sky Books
Detroit, Michigan

"No greater love, no greater joy, no further time, no other me…"

Your words (music, pencils, paints, motion, performances, songs, dreams, displays and soulful incantations) have weight. Your words (music, pencils, paints, motion, performances, songs, dreams, displays and soulful incantations) have truth. Your words (music, pencils, paints, motion, performances, songs, dreams, displays and soulful incantations) have meaning.

Notes on Where God Is

This is in no particular order, but it's hardly random. God is rarely in doggedly random decisions.

They tend to be loud and desperate.

Let us pray…

We pray -

For the silent spaces

We pray for the daily graces

We deal cards

(but hide the aces)

Looking to find the finish line;

Somebody: tell us where the race is.

How we treat silence says a lot about us, how we love, how we fear or wish, how we sing to angels who never seem to hear. Silence's gold has become a veneer. Purity is for sale to noise, and noise is meant only for confusion.

We should heed the example of our Gods. They are quiet unless there seems a need to speak that someone may hear. To touch, to smile, to sigh, to cry, to *live*... without a thousand voices forever shouting.

Is it too quiet? When a camera-ready smile follows earthquake casualty reports, do you care? Can you really? H'lo? There's Jesus over there quietly resurrecting, spectacle free, lonely, wondering why not a single news crew is anywhere around.

Dramatic footage required. Of Buddha. Of Goddess. Of Husband. Of Wife.

Where is **GOD** in the 21st century? Where is that ineffable, inescapable feeling of being *alive?* Dates may change but believe me, we are locked in fallacy. Until the screeching noises abate we'll be victims of our news forever.

Welcome to the 21st Century

Insert your own powerful prayer for peace and quiet.

Notes on where God is.

Somewhere inside the 21st Century

What do you worship?

God ain't in the paycheck, even though for most of us it's about the quietest thing we own.

God is in the quiet spaces.

God is not in the details;
the devil's in the details.
God is in the quiet spaces.

God is most definitely in squeezing a
balloon to make it bulge out the
other side of your fist.

God is not in me. Not now.
Not today.

(I am angry)
(and full of primitive needs)

This, too, shall pass.

God is not in fearful compassion,
God is in fear distilled to a purity
to be sought after.

There are times a body just wants to stare out the window at unmoving, barren trees before ever thinking about engaging the wider world, particularly when the sky is thought-grey, the wind barely a cat's passage, and there's nothing particularly on one's mind. Waking up like that leads to all kinds of thoughts of creativity and communion. You want to invite a god to jump under the covers and enjoy that ever-living warmth with you. This is what it feels like to be everything and nothing, and in that feeling feel fine. I wrote this while trees pretended they weren't staring into my room; while a tiny space heater hummed; while the world waited for me to get up. I finally got up. I finally engaged the wide world. Good morning.

When's the last time you laughed
without caring what you looked like,
how you sounded,
where you were,
or what others thought?

Just wondering.

Because…

Lord love a duck.

God is not in the city. In the city, if not for the sky, you wouldn't even know you were on a planet.

God is in conquering fears.

Crumbling corn bread on greens has to
be part of a holy ritual somewhere.

God is leaning back in a chair anywhere in the world with a smile on your face after talking to your mother.

God is in every book you ever read and were confident the writer honestly wanted to tell you something.

God is in the secrets.

God waits for you outside church. He's patient. He can wait till you're done.

Had Bob Marley sing:
"Mighty God is a living man!"

So don't leave God stranded in the parking lot after services. Even a patient man eventually wants to be offered a ride home.

There are times when even God doesn't understand and looks to you for guidance.

Can you find what's in your mind?

God is in the sculptured archway of an art museum, its solid wrought-iron gateway of petrified vines, leaves, birds and artful curlicues, but not in the museum itself.

God is in twigs if you pick them up.
A twig not held is not God.

God is not in the lazy, sullen
Flotsam in our water.

(Oh, and God likes to barbecue nearly
every day. No relation. Just thought
you'd like to know.)

God is in lemonade when it's cooled,
refreshing, and not too sweet.

God is in a discussion of logic
with your children.

God is in guitars, but
God doesn't rock.
God transcends rock.
God is funk rock.
God is flamenco.
God is mariachi.

God is acoustic. And bass that makes your eyes widen and your breath catch when bass is played that good. Do you understand that God is a guitar? Prince, Jimi, Carlos, Satriani, Flea, Isley, Morello – Preach on.

God is not in the designer labels in
which you profess to care.
Nope, not there.
Left a message though: *Life is casual.*

God is in telling it like it is and
it *is* like it is.

God is not in **love** for the sake of **love**
but **love** so that others can **love** you too.

God cannot be in a gun.

D
R
E
A
M
I
N
G

IS

FREE

God is in smiling.

God is in running fast, running faster, faster, running **fast**…and then you suddenly *stop!*

The slap of that foot is God.

God is **always** alone with you.

God is not in the practice of law.

God is in apples.
And grapes.
And mangoes.
And pineapples.
And Asian pears.
And sweet pickles.
And navel oranges.
But not kumquats.
Nobody knows what's in there.

God is a shark.

Insert your own powerful prayer
for peace and quiet.

God is in the end of the day.

God is in sometimes arousing somebody
without intending to.

Gently rocking in a swing, feet touching the ground, alone with your thoughts. Maybe you're worrying about a relative. Maybe it's been a while since you've seen a willow.

God is in the park in the early morning before the people who never get enough attention get there.

God is in the aroma of a
barbecue fire.
I think you knew that, though.

God is not in trying to get attention out
of slothful boredom.

Hey there, Lonely Person

Don't you know my heart is
meant for you?

Importance diminished is not God.

Ate an apple with God on a bright spring day. We talked about things we'd done in a familiar way. I was ashamed to admit anger at my lot. God was amused at the feelings I've got. In this bag of apples lives grass under a parking lot, lives the rain when the world's too hot, lives the never empty pot. The grass tickled the small of my back; tickled my thoughts of where I was at: against a tree, home where I belong. And if no one saw God I am here to tell you that: Her smile is much clearer than fact; God is the reason, the season, the storm; the truthful back when you're tired and worn. God and I ate apples. In this bag of apples lives grass under a parking lot, lives the rain when the sun is too hot, lives the wisdom of the never empty pot. The never empty pot. God and I ate apples on the edge of a parking lot.

Fantasy is reality at its best. How often would you imagine God fantasizes about you?

There are too many people in this world ready and willing to cause you pain.

The person who says they love you shouldn't be one of them.

Who loves you, baby?

"We're all the ones who know so little,
and I'm the one you least need to fear."

Write it down. Read it aloud.

Embrace y'self.

God is in wondering
what certain things mean.

God is in the woman I see on Belle Isle in the black and red tracksuit power-walking with such a magnificent and confident stride. She is alone. She wears no music. She hears the wind. She feels the rush that she creates, but there is no rush. No matter how long it takes, time is on her side.

God likes to fish without worrying
whether or not He's going to
catch anything.

God is in birdcalls when there's
no other noise around.

Once again: Release it. It ain't your
friend. Yes, again. Here. Now.
We'll wait.

Come on, now.

God absolutely lives
for telling a loved one
to stop being a fool.

God is the way huge tankers cut through waters like ancient aquatic dinosaurs— but only when those tankers are seen from on land.

God is in recalling the pride of learning
something important on your own.

Of course, on hot days shade is God.

A woman feeds ducks from the palm of her hand from time to time. The absent way she returns a lock of hair to its comfortable place behind her ear is reminiscent of something.

God is in being able to whistle along with the parts of songs that have whistling in them.

God is music. *Composition* is God.

How about this: sometimes I feel a certain breeze that seems to want my attention and waits on it patiently. When I finally note its presence it blows just a little harder, slides down my collar to cool. Then a big bug flies by; I do a jerky panic dance to avoid it, almost falling off the porch. A private, unembarrassed smile is on my face when I sit back down. And there's that breeze again.

It's actually quite simple: *violence ain't God;* killing ain't God; war ain't God. If you heard otherwise, they lied to you. Get your money back, then go find some reality.

At no charge.

Nope, not in computers.
They compete with God too much.

God is not in architecture that denies
life. There must be breath, there must be
flow.

God is in the moments you have without getting in your own way… *Move!*

God is in taking a break from your problems without forgetting to head back to them.

Walking around University where I put myself through college is definitely a holy endeavor. Today is Sunday, the campus is quiet, but folks still walk its beautiful grounds; students reflect on how their week went (one is holding a puppy while the other idly talks); a young mother lets her daughter play on the grass of the dorm lawn; I'm glad to see more trees have been planted throughout. My vantage is before two particularly romantic trees, two of the older ones crossing one another with the upper reaches so entangled neither knows its true end. As long as they remember where they began. I'm gladdened by the diversity of styles, cultures, and attitudes I see here; by old folks with book bags. Gladdened as well by a common factor: quietude. No impositions. No voices carry. No glances linger. Beauty is allowed its respect, the beauty of women, men, nature and privacy. Monday there'll be hustle and bustle, voices will carry, looks will linger out of curiosity and desire, but all still within the context of the non-deviating path. I could stay here forever.

Fact

Truth

Joy

Antithesis

Creation

Bounty

Such colorful words.

…at times I feel like a rainbow.

God is not the absence of a life.

Experience deliciously innocent flirtation especially when you're madly in love.

It comes highly recommended.

Pity is the absence of God;
compassionate hope the epitome.

God contradicts.

God laughs while doing so.

There's a fair amount of God in massive construction equipment preparing to chew into the ground under the steady guidance of fragile bones and skin in anticipation of some grand, magnificent structure. It will be a shrine for all that enter, whether they worship or not.

There's a line: "The mixture of a lie doth
ever add pleasure."

Read *Of Truth,*
Sir Francis Bacon, author.

Men are not God if they must be "men."
Of defining moments
there are precious few.

Children. No children are too cute to be God. Children are the devil with amnesia. Little confused birthed souls— make them happy in their new life.

Let them become gods.

God is in the infinite, perfect clarity of honesty.

This world is built on pain—
but what of the good?

Go back to page one and start over.
I don't think you hear me.

If God saw what you did would
He call your mama?
Would she even care,
that's the question?

For some reason God is in the number
three thousand eight hundred and twelve.

God is inside me.
She makes her way farther out.

God is inside me. He calls… I don't hear. He shouts…

…I look up.

There are certain times of day.

Ten minutes before bedtime, talking quietly in the dark about the first day you met. Sunset on Friday. The 1:30 pm breeze during a weekend in the garden. The office before anyone else arrives to wonder why you're sitting there with no lights on. Such comfort.

God is in suspense, not terror. Comedy,
not stupidity. Drama, not contrivance.
He wrote all of Shakespeare's works.

We pray to God to make Him infallible.
Practice makes perfect.

God has never tried to sell me anything.
The Devil, though, *loves* commercials.

I don't usually let anger in. Today I let anger in and gave it a home. Dear Lord, forgive me.

Some idiotic, nameless, faceless person cut me off on the road.

I imagined a fist crushing the ice from his soul.

Dear Lord. What have I become?

I know the suffering of others is supposed to lead to a change in me, but I'd rather not be made an example of, thank you.

That ineffably inescapable feeling of
being alive…

…is in a billion other places you might
not have thought to look.

I think sweet potato pie just might be
God in disguise.

Think. Think. No, not the way you're thinking. *Think!* Without worrying about who's looking.

Take your time; we won't leave you behind.

I'll say this twice 'cause I don't think you hear me: (1) BE GOOD TO EACH OTHER; (2) BE GOOD FOR EACH OTHER. Unless both conditions are met, sorry to say that love, *sweet love,* is not love. That word has power; don't use it in vain. Love. If I had time I'd tell everybody. Call it the secret formula of love, put it in a one-page book and there'd never be another relationship manual printed ever again. One page love: *be good to each other; be good for each other.* There ain't no half way.

Ah, I understand now. You thought Life wasn't supposed to be simple. No joy in random causalities. Baby, baby, baby— don't listen to the TV, the movies, the songs, the badly written books, noooo. They're just after that stuff in your pocket that claims "In God We Trust." They're the ones proclaiming there's no such thing as a real life.

We're almost at the end.

Here it is

God is not interested in yes men. God says listen to rock and eat empanadas and laugh at the lewd jokes your best friend tells and read cheesy romance novels and study physics and make love as though trying to touch the face of glory and object when you need to and never belittle a child and be the right kind of selfish for the right kind of reasons and get your mind, body, your soul in order 'cause every house is the house of the Lord and never pray without doing and remember that in life the story you think you're telling is never the one that's being told and accept more than one name for God and before you say "I am what I am" be who you are and don't be afraid, don't be afraid, don't be afraid…of the quiet spaces. Blessed be the private places without a thousand voices, places where

angels and saints will call you by name.
Maybe offer you some lemonade.

There are a thousand voices shouting.
Except one. Now another.

Then another…

Please. Insert your own powerful
prayers for peace.

Here.

Time

Time…

...is your friend.

Made in the USA
Middletown, DE
28 January 2017